Sign Language & Clothing

Bela Davis

Abdo Kids Junior
is an Imprint of Abdo Kids
abdobooks.com

Abdo
EVERYDAY SIGN LANGUAGE
Kids

MW00957041

abdobooks.com

Published by Abdo Kids, a division of ABDO, P.O. Box 398166, Minneapolis, Minnesota 55439.
Copyright © 2023 by Abdo Consulting Group, Inc. International copyrights reserved in all countries.
No part of this book may be reproduced in any form without written permission from the publisher.
Abdo Kids Junior™ is a trademark and logo of Abdo Kids.

Printed in the United States of America, North Mankato, Minnesota.

102022

012023

THIS BOOK CONTAINS
RECYCLED MATERIALS

Photo Credits: Getty Images, Shutterstock, ©Sadie the dog p.17

Production Contributors: Teddy Borth, Jennie Forsberg, Grace Hansen

Design Contributors: Candice Keimig, Pakou Moua

Library of Congress Control Number: 2022937162

Publisher's Cataloging-in-Publication Data

Names: Davis, Bela, author.

Title: Sign language & clothing / by Bela Davis

Description: Minneapolis, Minnesota : Abdo Kids, 2023 | Series: Everyday sign language | Includes online
    resources and index.

Identifiers: ISBN 9781098264079 (lib. bdg.) | ISBN 9781098264635 (ebook) | ISBN 9781098264918
    (Read-to-Me ebook)

Subjects: LCSH: American Sign Language--Juvenile literature. | Clothing--Juvenile literature. | Deaf--
    Means of communication--Juvenile literature. | Language acquisition--Juvenile literature.

Classification: DDC 419--dc23

Table of Contents

Signs and Clothing

ASL is a visual language. There is a sign for all your favorite clothes!

CLOTHES

1. Make the "5" sign with both hands by spreading all fingers apart

2. Bring both hands to the upper chest

3. Quickly brush hands downward twice, tips of thumbs can touch the chest

Anna wore her favorite

dress today!

DRESS

1. Make the "5" sign with both hands by spreading all fingers apart

2. Bring both hands to the upper chest

3. Brush hands down and then out, like a dress would hang on the body

Liam's shirt has

stripes on it.

SHIRT

1. Use the index finger and thumb to grab your shirt in the upper chest area

2. Tug outward a few times

9

Jess is good at tying

her shoes.

SHOES

1. Make the "S" sign with both hands
2. Tap the fists together laterally two times

11

Gabe got new white pants!

PANTS

1. Place both hands in an open position just below the waist, palms facing in

2. Move both hands up to the waist

3. As the hands come up, bend the knuckles, and curl fingers up a bit

4. It should look like you are pulling up a pair of pants

Maya likes her

mismatched socks.

SOCKS

1. Using both hands, tuck in all fingers except for the index fingers
2. Point both index fingers downward
3. Rub the index fingers together a few times by moving them back and forth

Sadie likes to wear a coat when it is cold.

COAT

1. Make the "A" sign with both hands
2. Touch the thumbs to the shoulders
3. Move the hands downward and inward as if putting on a coat

17

Jen's favorite part of her costume is the hat.

HAT

1. With an open, dominant hand, pat the top of the head twice

19

The snowman is very

pleased with his gloves.

GLOVES

1. Hold open hands out in front, palms facing down
2. Slide the fingers of the dominant hand over the non-dominant hand, then do the reverse
3. It should look like you are putting on a pair of gloves

The ASL Alphabet!

Glossary

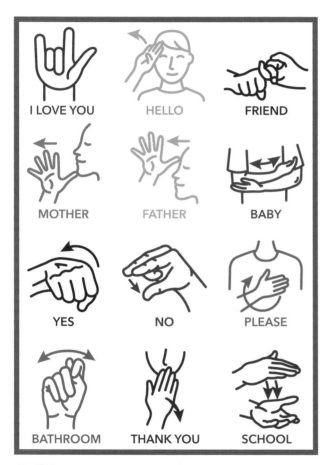

costume

clothing worn to make one look like some other person, animal, or thing.

mismatched

wrongly matched.

Index

Abdo Kids ONLINE
FREE! ONLINE MULTIMEDIA RESOURCES

Visit **abdokids.com** to access crafts, games, videos, and more!

Use Abdo Kids code **ESK4079** or scan this QR code!